ALTERNATIVE ENERGY

HYDROGEN FUEL CELLS

by Meg Marquardt

Content Consultant
Travis J. Williams
Associate Professor of Chemistry
University of Southern California

Core Library

An Imprint of Abdo Publishing
abdopublishing.com

abdopublishing.com

Published by Abdo Publishing, a division of ABDO, PO Box 398166, Minneapolis, Minnesota 55439. Copyright © 2017 by Abdo Consulting Group, Inc. International copyrights reserved in all countries. No part of this book may be reproduced in any form without written permission from the publisher. Core Library™ is a trademark and logo of Abdo Publishing.

Printed in the United States of America, North Mankato, Minnesota
092016
012017

Cover Photo: Tony Farrugia/Alamy
Interior Photo: Tony Farrugia/Alamy, 1; Shizuo Kambayashi/AP Images, 4, 45; Tom Myers/ Science Source, 7; AP Images, 9; Science Source, 10, 32; Richard Kail/Science Source, 12; Martyn F. Chillmaid/Science Source, 15; Everett Historical/Shutterstock Images, 17; Royal Institution of Great Britain/Science Source, 19; Shutterstock Images, 20, 37; Friedrich Saurer/ Science Source, 22; Chris Knapton/Science Source, 25, 43; Spencer Sutton/Science Source, 27; Martin Bond/Science Source, 29, 39; Yoshikazu Tsuno/AFP/Getty Images, 35

Editor: Arnold Ringstad
Series Designer: Nikki Farinella

Publisher's Cataloging-in-Publication Data

Names: Marquardt, Meg, author.
Title: Hydrogen fuel cells / by Meg Marquardt.
Description: Minneapolis, MN : Abdo Publishing, 2017. | Series: Alternative
    energy | Includes bibliographical references and index.
Identifiers: LCCN 2016945421 | ISBN 9781680784565 (lib. bdg.) |
    ISBN 9781680798418 (ebook)
Subjects: LCSH: Hydrogen as fuel--Juvenile literature. | Fuel cells--Juvenile
    literature. | Renewable energy sources--Juvenile literature.
Classification: DDC 665.8--dc23
LC record available at http://lccn.loc.gov/2016945421

CONTENTS

THE QUIET ALTERNATIVE

As the car zips down the highway, it is quiet. There is no grumble of a gasoline-powered engine. The exhaust does not spew out dirty smoke. The only sound is the tires on the road.

This is not some magical car of the future. It simply uses a hydrogen fuel cell instead of gasoline. A hydrogen fuel cell creates electricity from hydrogen gas. This electricity powers the car. Cars that use

Cars powered by hydrogen fuel cells look just like their gasoline counterparts from the outside.

gasoline emit carbon dioxide. Carbon dioxide is a greenhouse gas. It contributes to climate change.

Hydrogen fuel cell cars, however, have no dangerous emissions. The only by-product of a hydrogen engine is water. These cars can be an environmentally friendly alternative to gasoline cars.

By the 2010s, many cars powered by hydrogen fuel cells were in testing. A few were already driving around cities. But they were a long way from becoming available for everyday consumers.

Hydrogen Fuel on the Rise

The idea of using hydrogen to power vehicles goes back to the 1700s. At that time,

The First Hydrogen Flight

In 1783 the first hydrogen balloon climbed into the sky. French physicist Jacques Charles had watched other attempts to lift balloons with heated air. Charles decided to use hydrogen instead. His balloon climbed to more than 3,000 feet (900 m). It floated along for 15 miles (24 km). More than a century before the first airplane, the balloon carried passengers into the sky.

Under the hood, cars powered by fuel cells differ significantly from fossil fuel cars.

hydrogen was used to lift balloons. The gas is less dense than the air around it. A balloon filled with hydrogen could carry a person into the sky. But energy demands have changed a lot since then. Hydrogen is useful for more than its lifting power. Now it is being used to power cars and trucks.

Hydrogen fuel cells show a lot of promise. However, they also face hurdles. Fuel cells are expensive. Since each car would require several cells, the cars would be expensive.

In addition to money, other problems stand in

Hydrogen Economy

Hydrogen economy is a term used to describe all the parts of hydrogen energy production. This includes generating hydrogen, creating fuel cells, and storing the fuel. A hydrogen economy is about more than just money. It is also about a clean environment. Hydrogen fuel is supposed to be a clean source of energy. However, generating hydrogen takes energy. Sometimes the process is powered by dirty fuels, such as coal. Renewable energy sources, such as wind or solar, can create a stronger, cleaner hydrogen economy.

Until the 1930s, hydrogen was used to lift massive airships.

the way of a hydrogen-powered future. One is making enough hydrogen. It takes energy to produce the gas. Also, many hydrogen fuel cells are unable to make enough electricity to drive very long distances. A lot of the energy they produce is not turned into useable electricity. Another key issue is storage. Tanks must store a lot of hydrogen safely at high pressure.

More hydrogen filling stations will be needed for fuel cell cars to become popular.

And there are few hydrogen filling stations. Until all of these problems are fixed, hydrogen fuel cells can't replace gasoline.

But scientists are hard at work improving the technology. From creating new fuel tanks to building more filling stations, researchers hope to make hydrogen cars popular. There are challenges ahead, but scientists and car companies are up to the task.

EXPLORE ONLINE

Chapter One discusses hydrogen fuel cells as an alternative energy source. But hydrogen fuel cell cars are not the only alternative vehicles on the road. There are many other alternatives. Each has pros and cons. The website below lists several types of alternative vehicles. Which seem the most promising to you?

The Pros and Cons of Alternative Energy
mycorelibrary.com/hydrogen-fuel-cells

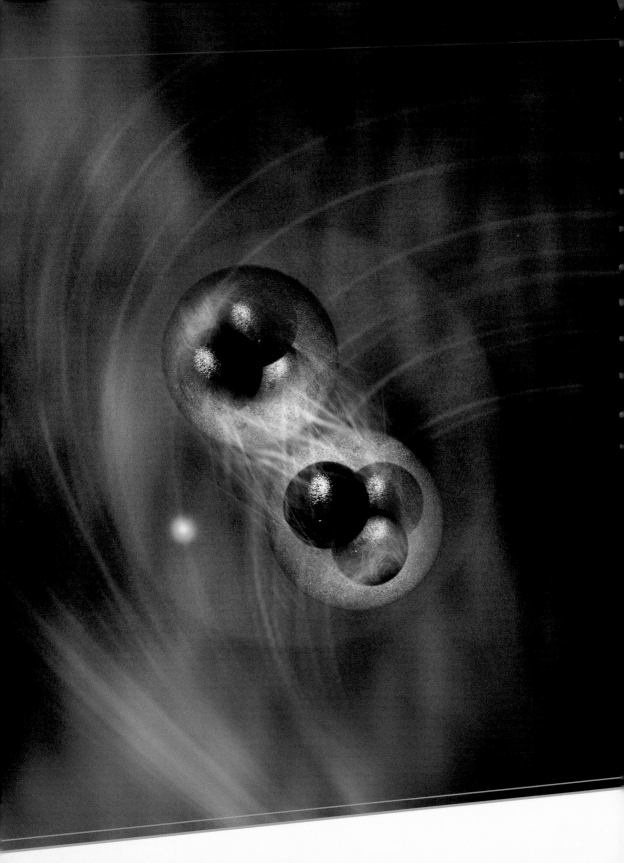

CHAPTER TWO

HYDROGEN HISTORY

The story of hydrogen fuel started hundreds of years ago. First, scientists had to discover hydrogen. Before the 1500s, people thought air was all made up of a single substance. They knew that rocks had many elements in them, such as silver or iron. But the air did not have any elements scientists could see.

Hydrogen is the most abundant element in the universe, yet it took scientists hundreds of years to fully understand it.

Hydrogen, the First Element

The periodic table is a list of all known elements. On the periodic table, hydrogen has the number one position. That is not because it was the first element ever discovered. People knew about elements such as gold and silver long before hydrogen. Instead, elements on the periodic table are organized by atomic number. An atomic number is the number of protons that are in each atom of an element. Hydrogen has only one proton. Therefore, it has the first position on the table.

Paracelsus first realized that different sorts of air might exist. Paracelsus was a scientist who lived in the 1500s. While iron was dissolved in an acid, he realized it gave off something strange. But at the time, the idea of a gas did not yet exist.

A century later, things had changed. Scientists had done many experiments with burning metals. Some kinds of air could catch fire. Some gave metals strange properties. Flemish chemist Jan Baptista van Helmont was the first to use the word *gas*.

A laboratory reaction between metal and acid, left, can be used to produce hydrogen.

Robert Boyle performed experiments with iron and acid in 1671. He knew he was producing some sort of gas, but he could not identify it. In the 1700s, Henry Cavendish proved there were different kinds of gas. He named the gas Boyle found *inflammable air*. In 1783 Antoine Lavoisier named this gas hydrogen.

Using Hydrogen for Fuel

Gases often had curious properties. Some were less dense than others. Researchers realized that gases less dense than air could float. By the late 1700s, hydrogen balloons had taken to the sky.

However, these balloons were difficult or impossible to steer. Inventors were hard at work creating an airship that might be easier to handle. By the early 1900s airships were able to cross the Atlantic Ocean. Engines with propellers pushed the ships through the air.

Still, hydrogen was hard to work with. In the early balloons, hydrogen gas was produced with the same method Robert Boyle had used. Iron filings were melted with acid to produce the gas. But this is a slow way of making hydrogen. It could take days to fill the balloon.

The process was dangerous too. Hydrogen gas is flammable. It can catch fire and explode very easily. All of that gas floating around in the balloon was a fire hazard. In 1937 a giant airship called the *Hindenburg* burned up as it tried to land. The incident brought the use of hydrogen in balloons to an end.

The *Hindenburg* disaster showed the potential dangers of hydrogen.

The *Hindenburg* Disaster

Hydrogen explosions plagued the airship industry in the 1930s. It was such a danger that many designers looked for a different gas. Helium was a good alternative. However, the United States was the leading producer of helium. It did not want to give that helium to other countries. The *Hindenburg* was a German ship. It flew with hydrogen. On May 6, 1937, the airship exploded into flames while it tried to land in New Jersey. The disaster killed 35 people in the airship and one person on the ground.

Creating Fuel Cells

As inventors built hydrogen balloons, scientists learned more about the gas. Their discoveries would change the history of hydrogen forever.

Scientists discovered hydrogen is part of water. Each molecule of water is made up of two hydrogen atoms and one oxygen atom. By the 1800s, researchers had figured out how to split water into hydrogen and oxygen. But when they tried to do the reverse, the result was surprising. Not only was water produced, but so was

In addition to his work on fuel cells, Grove also researched early batteries and photography technology.

electricity. In 1839 William Grove created a device to carry out this reaction. It was the first fuel cell.

This use of hydrogen fuel was much different from what came before. Previously, balloons used hydrogen's low density to fly. Now hydrogen gas could be used to generate electricity. This electricity could power machines. But there was a

Gasoline-powered cars have been the most popular form of transportation for more than 100 years.

major problem. The process did not produce enough energy to be useful.

By the mid-1800s, the internal combustion engine had been invented. These engines ran on gasoline. They were very powerful and efficient. They were used in the vast majority of cars. Despite hydrogen's advantages, it had a long way to go before it could compete with gasoline.

FURTHER EVIDENCE

Chapter Two discusses the discovery and early use of hydrogen. But even in its early uses, it was a difficult gas to handle. What evidence can you find to support this point? In modern vehicles, hydrogen is still a challenge to use. Go to the website below. Write down a few reasons why hydrogen gas is difficult to use today. Compare and contrast these reasons to the early difficulties with hydrogen.

Hydrogen Fuel
mycorelibrary.com/hydrogen-fuel-cells

CHAPTER THREE

HOW FUEL CELLS WORK

A hydrogen fuel cell is made up of electrodes, electrolytes, and catalysts. These parts take advantage of the movement of tiny particles inside atoms called electrons to generate electricity.

Inside a Fuel Cell

Electrons are negatively charged particles. As they move from one place to another, they can produce electricity. Their negative charge means they are

Particles invisible to the naked eye make fuel cell technology possible.

attracted to positive charges. Sometimes this charge is another particle. In a fuel cell, it is usually a positively charged electrode.

Each cell has two different electrodes. One is an anode. An anode is negatively charged. It produces electrons. The other is a cathode. A cathode is positively charged. Electrons move from the anode to the cathode.

In the space between electrodes is an electrolyte. Electrolytes can be made up of solids or liquids. Only certain types of particles can move through an electrolyte. Electrons cannot. They must find another path to the cathode. The path they are forced to take leads to a circuit. That is where the electricity is generated.

Catalysts are things that help speed up a reaction. In fuel cells, catalysts are often used to break hydrogen atoms into protons and electrons. Different catalysts are used depending on the type of fuel cell and the type of electrodes used.

Scientists are studying fuel cells in their labs to improve efficiency and make them more useful.

How Hydrogen Makes Electricity

These basic parts are found in all fuel cells. Different types of fuel cells contain a variety of other components. But many also feature two more things in common: hydrogen and oxygen.

Hydrogen gas is pumped into the cell on the anode side. The anode has a catalyst, such as platinum. Each hydrogen molecule contains two hydrogen atoms. Each of these atoms has one proton and one electron. The catalyst ionizes the atoms, dividing the molecule into its protons and electrons. The protons go across the electrolyte. The electrons cannot pass through the electrolyte. Instead they flow through the circuit. The protons and electrons all end up at the cathode.

Powering More Than Cars

Hydrogen fuel cells have other uses besides cars. Researchers are looking into portable cells to use in small devices, such as power tools. They are also thinking about bigger uses. In 2009 the US Navy used a hydrogen fuel cell to power an unmanned aerial vehicle, an aircraft without a pilot.

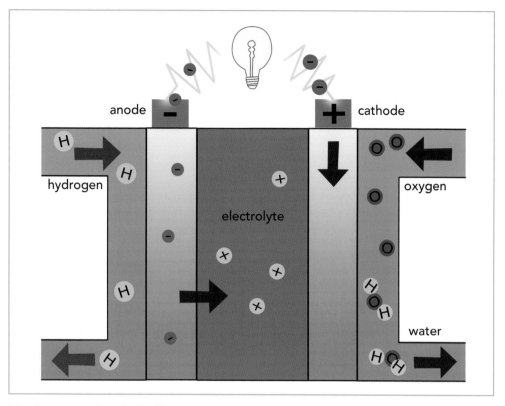

Hydrogen Fuel Cell

Above is a diagram of how a fuel cell works. How does the diagram help you understand how a fuel cell operates?

On the cathode side, oxygen is fed into the cell. As the hydrogen's electrons and protons reach the cathode, they bind with the oxygen to make water. In the process, some heat is given off. The fuel cell reaction only has three by-products: electricity, water, and heat.

Hydrogen Fuel Cells and Safety

When people think of a hydrogen-powered vehicle, they may think about the danger of this inflammable gas exploding. But hydrogen fuel cell cars are designed to be very safe. The tanks are made of carbon fiber, a durable material. In a test, a tank even withstood bullets being shot at it. Plus, the cars are built with smart technology. If sensors detect a hydrogen leak, the whole system shuts down. With everything turned off, there's nothing that can cause a spark. No spark means no explosion.

Problems with Fuel Cells

The science seems simple. But the reality of fuel cells has proven challenging. There are a lot of different types of fuel cells. They are often named for the type of electrolyte that is used. For example, some fuel cells use metal compounds as an electrolyte. Another type uses phosphoric acid. Different electrolytes give fuel cells different properties. Some work at different temperatures. Some are more expensive to make than others.

The limitations of fuel cells have meant they have mainly been used in experimental vehicles, such as this boat.

Expense is a major reason why fuel cell cars are not yet popular. Some cells are more efficient than others. Some do not produce enough energy to be practical. And fuel storage is also a major challenge. Researchers have had difficulties storing enough hydrogen to drive a car long distances. However, these challenges have not stopped scientists and engineers from pursuing new advances in hydrogen fuel cells.

Ulf Bossel is a scientist who specializes in fuel cell technology. He notes that making hydrogen takes a lot of electricity. This means the gas is really carrying energy from one place to another, rather than serving as a source of energy itself:

> The advantages of hydrogen praised by journalists (non-toxic, burns to water, abundance of hydrogen in the Universe, etc.) are misleading, because the production of hydrogen depends on the availability of energy and water, both of which are increasingly rare and may become political issues, as much as oil and natural gas are today. . . . Ultimately, hydrogen has to be made from renewable electricity by electrolysis of water in the beginning, and then its energy content is converted back to electricity with fuel cells when it's recombined with oxygen to water. Separating hydrogen from water by electrolysis requires massive amounts of electrical energy and substantial amounts of water.

> Source: Lisa Zyga. "Why a Hydrogen Economy Doesn't Make Sense." Phys.org. Phys.org, December 11, 2016. Web. July 25, 2016

Back It Up

Bossel is using evidence to support his point. Write a sentence about what Bossel's main point is. Then write down two or three pieces of evidence he uses.

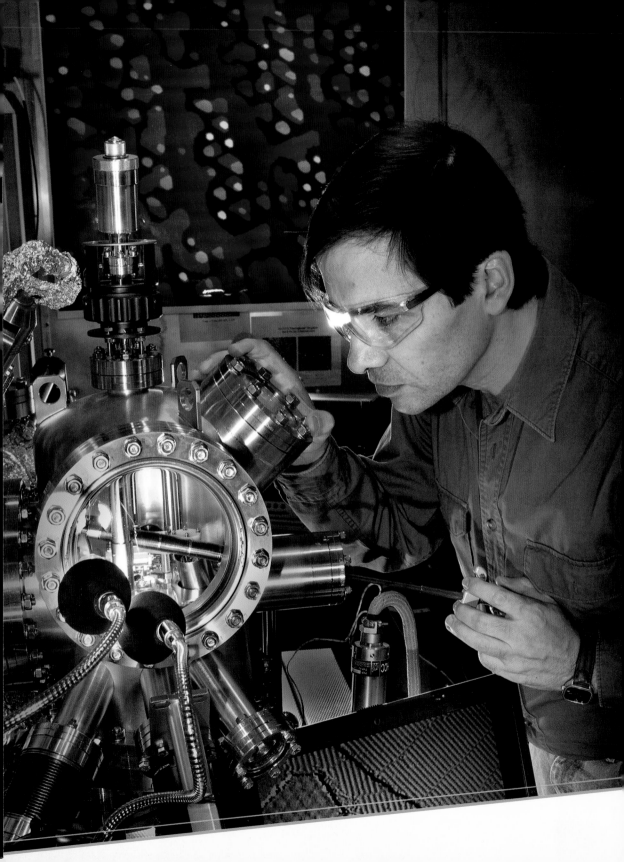

THE FUTURE OF HYDROGEN

More than 200 years after early hydrogen balloons, hydrogen-powered travel is still not popular. However, fuel cell technology is getting better and better. And it is also getting cheaper to produce. Still, many challenges lie ahead.

Hydrogen fuel cells use expensive materials. One of the biggest expenses is the catalyst, which

Scientists are researching new catalysts in labs all over the world.

contains platinum. Platinum enables the cell's chemical reactions. It is good at what it does. But it is expensive. Scientists are looking for ways to replace platinum. Iron, cobalt, and carbon have been studied as alternatives. Using these materials could bring costs down.

The Problem of Storage

Storage is one of the biggest challenges for using hydrogen in cars. Hydrogen holds much less energy than gasoline by volume. That means in order to go as far as gasoline allows, a hydrogen fuel tank would need to be bigger.

A large tank is impractical. One way around the problem is to use compression tanks. Compression tanks could fit more hydrogen gas into a smaller volume. Another idea is to use liquid hydrogen tanks. Liquid hydrogen could then be turned back into a gas. But both of those systems have their own challenges. Scientists are still working to figure out the right materials to use when building these types of tanks.

Factory workers install a hydrogen tank in a fuel cell vehicle.

Hydrogen is only a liquid when it is below −423.2 degrees Fahrenheit (−252.9°C). A tank would have to withstand extremely cold temperatures. For compression systems, the material would need to be strong enough to handle extremely high pressures. The tank would also need to resist damage. Most fuel cells need very pure hydrogen. A tank that cracks or flakes would make the gas impure. Scientists are figuring out solutions to these problems.

One of the first available fuel cell cars is the Toyota Mirai. It uses two tanks strengthened with a tough material called carbon fiber. The tanks hold 11 pounds (5 kg) of hydrogen. It is stored at a pressure of 10,000 pounds per square inch (69 megapascals). The tanks are specially designed to remain safe in a crash.

Refueling Concerns

Like a gasoline-powered car, a hydrogen fuel car requires refueling. There are more than 150,000 gas stations nationwide. But by July 2016, there were only

Fueling Up on Hydrogen

If you have a hydrogen car, here are all the states where you can top off your tank. Take a look at the map. What is the biggest hurdle to making hydrogen cars available nationwide? What would be the best locations for more filling stations?

27 public hydrogen refueling stations in the United States. Twenty-four of them were in California.

Part of the problem is that demand is small. Without many hydrogen cars, there is little need for fuel stations. But without fuel stations, it is difficult to use a hydrogen car.

Hydrogen Refueling Stations

The biggest storage tanks at a hydrogen station can hold nearly 10,000 gallons (38,000 L) of liquid hydrogen. But these tanks aren't underground. They sit on the surface a safe distance from the pumps. The liquid hydrogen is converted to a gas. Refilling a hydrogen tank is not quite like using a gasoline pump. The refill is automatic. The pumping stations are smart, meaning they can read just how much hydrogen to pump. Filling a tank may take up to five minutes.

Another issue is that with so few hydrogen cars on the road, it is difficult to know just what sort of fueling system to put into place. Since most stations are already in California, most early hydrogen cars have been used there. But it is unclear how many stations are needed and how far apart to place them.

Hydrogen Fuel on the Horizon

Hydrogen fuel burns cleanly. The tailpipes of hydrogen fuel cell cars give off water rather than dangerous gases. Just like solar or wind energy, hydrogen fuel cells are an alternative energy source.

Some buses in London, England, are powered by hydrogen fuel cells.

Carbon Free?

Hydrogen fuel cells do not produce any greenhouse gases. But that does not mean they're completely carbon free. It takes energy to get hydrogen from water. That process can produce greenhouse gases. Also, hydrogen has to be transported from production sites. Currently, that transportation is done using vehicles that produce greenhouse gases. It will take some time before transportation trucks could be powered by hydrogen as well.

Their use might help cut down on pollution. But they are not quite ready to take the place of fossil fuels. Scientists have a lot of challenges ahead of them. Still, the reality of hydrogen fuel is closer than ever before.

Though many people are in favor of hydrogen cars, some are not quite sure. Levi Tillemann, an energy expert, talked about the Toyota Mirai, one of the first hydrogen cars on the road:

> Generally hydrogen is produced through steam methane reforming (from natural gas), which means a lot of CO_2 emitted. The hydrogen needs to be stored either at very high pressures or cryogenically as a liquid—and all of that takes a lot of energy. In terms of greenhouse gas emissions, the Mirai is not much more efficient than your standard Prius—it's much worse than an electric car. . . . But the reasons I would continue to invest in hydrogen can be boiled down to one word: optionality. Addressing global warming will require a broad portfolio of clean energy technologies and in the long run we're not sure which ones will work best. Continuing to invest some risky money in hydrogen fuel cells actually makes a lot of sense. There may be a big payoff down the line.

Source: Levi Tillemann. "An Energy Expert's Love-Hate Affair with Toyota's Hydrogen Fuel Cell Mirai." Fortune. Fortune, May 13, 2015. Web. July 25, 2016.

What's the Big Idea?

Take a close look at this passage. What is the main point Tillemann is trying to make? How might hydrogen fuel cells fit in with the bigger energy picture?

- Hydrogen was first recognized as a distinct gas in the 1700s.
- William Grove created the first hydrogen fuel cell in 1839.
- Hydrogen fuel cells take in hydrogen gas, generating electricity and emitting water.
- Hydrogen fuel cells are more environmentally friendly than gasoline. They do not produce greenhouse gases.
- Hydrogen fuel cells can also be used to power vehicles such as planes and drones.
- Hydrogen can be stored in tanks and pumped into vehicles.
- Hydrogen is the most abundant element in the universe.
- Even with all of the challenges, some commercial hydrogen-powered cars are now available.
- Inside a fuel cell, electrons stripped from hydrogen molecules travel through a circuit, resulting in electricity. Oxygen then binds with the hydrogen molecules, creating water.

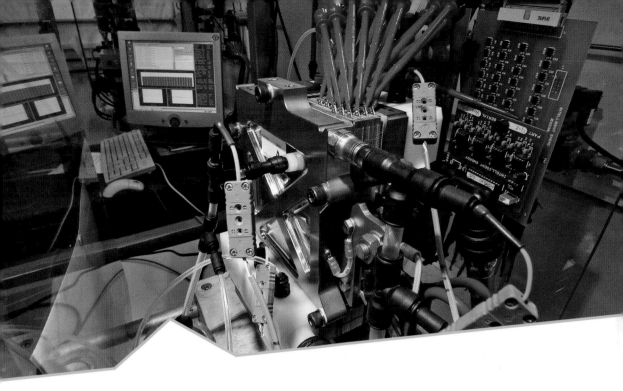

- Cost, efficiency, and storage are the major challenges facing hydrogen fuel cell technology.
- The first hydrogen-powered vessel was the *Globe*. It was a balloon that used hydrogen gas to lift itself into the air. It launched in France on August 27, 1783.

STOP AND THINK

You Are There

This book discusses traveling in a hydrogen balloon. Imagine you are one of the first people to take to the sky in one in the 1700s. Write a letter home talking about your adventures. What's it like rising into the sky? What other uses might this new gas have in the 1700s? Be sure to add plenty of detail to your notes.

Why Do I Care?

Maybe you do not have strong feelings about whether or not the world should use hydrogen fuel cells. But that doesn't mean you can't think about the different ways to help the world find new sources of energy. What other alternative energy sources can you think of? What pros or cons do they have compared to hydrogen fuel cells?

Dig Deeper

After reading this book, what questions do you still have about hydrogen fuel cells? With an adult's help, find a few reliable sources that can help you answer your questions. Write a paragraph about what you learned.

Surprise Me

Chapter Four discusses the many challenges that hydrogen power still faces. After reading this book, what two or three facts about hydrogen fuel cells did you find most surprising? Write a few sentences about each fact. Why did you find each fact surprising?

GLOSSARY

atom
a basic building block of matter

circuit
a closed path along which electricity can flow

density
a measure of a substance's mass divided by its volume

economy
the system by which goods and services are bought and sold

electron
a negatively charged subatomic particle

greenhouse gas
a gas that traps heat in the atmosphere, contributing to climate change

inflammable
able to be set on fire

ionize
to add or take away electrons from an atom, giving the atom a positive or negative charge

proton
a positively charged subatomic particle

LEARN MORE

Books

Bjornlund, Lydia. *What Is the Future of Alternative Energy Cars?* San Diego, CA: ReferencePoint, 2014.

Lippman, David. *Energy from Hydrogen.* Ann Arbor, MI: Cherry Lake, 2008.

Rigsby, Mike. *Doable Renewables: 16 Alternative Energy Projects for Young Scientists.* Chicago, IL: Chicago Review, 2010.

Websites

To learn more about Alternative Energy, visit **booklinks.abdopublishing.com**. These links are routinely monitored and updated to provide the most current information available.

Visit **mycorelibrary.com** for free additional tools for teachers and students.

INDEX

ABOUT THE AUTHOR

Meg Marquardt started as a scientist but decided she liked writing about science even more. She enjoys researching physics, geology, and climate science. She lives in Madison, Wisconsin, with her two scientist cats, Lagrange and Doppler.